MW00950911

This book belongs to...

_____

Be Prepared For Anything

Love Yourself First

Today I Am Grateful For...

This worksheet is designed to help you practice gratitude. Make as many copies as you'd like. The more you practice gratitude, the happier your life will be.

Something that happened to me recently that I am grateful for:

_____
_____
_____
_____
_____
_____
_____

Someone who is always there for me and I really appreciate:

_____
_____
_____

Someone I look up to and why:

_____
_____
_____
_____
_____
_____

The best thing that happened today:

_____
_____
_____
_____

Something that has made my life easier:

_____
_____
_____
_____
_____
_____

Someone I love spending time with and why:

_____
_____
_____
_____
_____

I smiled or belly laughed today because:

_____
_____
_____
_____
_____
_____

A song that makes me happy

_____
_____

Something I was able to do for someone else that made me happy:

_____
_____
_____

Something that has changed my life for the better in the past year and how it has impacted my life.

_____
_____
_____
_____
_____
_____
_____
_____

I'm looking forward to:

_____
_____
_____
_____
_____
_____

Simple pleasures I enjoy:

_____
_____
_____
_____

Something or someone that has inspired me and how:

_____
_____
_____
_____
_____
_____
_____
_____

Positive Thinking To Help Situational Depression

Negativity is often an overwhelming element of situational depression. For millions of people with this type of depression, the key to begin breaking free is to change the situation, when possible, and/or the way the situation is viewed.

What situation is contributing to or causing my depression?

_____

_____

_____

_____

Is the situation a result of my actions or choices? Explain.

_____

_____

_____

_____

What are the positive things I've learned due the experience?

_____

_____

_____

_____

If I could do it over again, this is what I would do differently:

_____

_____

_____

Is negative self-talk making my depression worse? Give examples:

_____

_____

_____

_____

I can change the negative thoughts and self-talk into positives like these:

_____

_____

_____

_____

I can alleviate my stress and depression by focusing on the positives such as:

_____

_____

_____

_____

When situations are not a result of my actions or choices and I have limited control over things, I need to take these steps to maintain a positive mindset:

_____

_____

_____

_____

If I need additional help staying positive or fighting back the depression, I can count on and contact these friends and professionals:

_____

_____

25 Positive Thinking Affirmations

Affirmations are simple reminders to our subconscious that tells it to stay positive and focused on reaching our goals. They are meant to be used for ourselves, not for others. Affirmations can create more appreciation for the things we have and are surrounded with. They can bring more joy and happiness to our lives.

When creating your affirmations, there are a few things to keep in mind.

- Including the words "I am" in your affirmations bring power to your statement.
- Positively state what you want, not what you don't want.
- Keep your statements short and specific.
- Include words that show action or emotion
- Before stating your affirmation, take a deep breath and focus on what you're saying.
- Be grateful for what you have, the people in your life and your surroundings.
- Let go of the past. You can't change it so don't waste time thinking on it.
- Celebrate your 'wins'.

Below are 25 positive thinking affirmations to get you started.

1. I can do better, just by deciding to do so.
2. Life is what I make of it.
3. I can.
4. I am above negative thoughts and actions.
5. Happiness is a choice. I choose it.
6. Today, I let go of old habits and take up new ones.
7. I am conquering obstacles every day.
8. I am seeing a positive in every situation.
9. My thoughts are becoming more positive each day.
10. Life is getting better all the time.
11. I am turning into the person I always wanted to be.
12. Thinking positive is starting to feel more natural to me.
13. My optimism is altering my reality.
14. I am at peace with my past and looking forward to the future.
15. I no longer fear tomorrow.
16. I am blessed.
17. This too shall pass.
18. I control how I feel.
19. I am willing to do what it takes to make positive changes.
20. The future is mine, if I choose to take it.
21. I am indestructible.
22. This moment is awesome.
23. Positive thinking is part of who I am now.
24. Today is the first day of my new life.
25. Everything happens for a reason that serves me.

Every step that I take to move forward allows me to grow stronger by the day.

30 Ways to Think More Positively

After years of having a fixed, negative mindset, it's tough to change one's ways. But with practice, you can create a more positive outlook on life. Here's 30 ways to practice thinking more positively.

1. When talking, replace negative words with positive words. Instead of saying "This is too hard", say "I can do this" or "I accept this challenge".

2. When thinking, use empowering words; those that make you feel strong, happy, motivated and in control.

3. Journal your thoughts. Celebrate your successes. Document and analyze the losses. Find where you went wrong and plan to do better next time. Learn from your mistakes.

4. Counter each negative thought with multiple positive thoughts. When you catch yourself having negative thoughts, take a moment to think two or three positive thoughts.

5. Go somewhere that brings you peace and happiness. This might be a nature walk, a quiet place like a museum that is visually appealing, an area where you listen to music, a park where you can watch kids and pets play happily. As often as possible, visit this place where you feel peace and happiness.

6. Practice positive affirmations. The more you practice, the easier it will become.

7. Forgive yourself for missteps. It happens. The important this is not to dwell on them and keep moving forward.

8. Surround yourself with positive people.

9. Add inspiring visuals and colors to your home and work space.

10. Look at things from a different point of view. When you can see both sides, you can eliminate a lot of negatively.

11. Laugh aloud and often. There's always something to laugh about. Smiling and laughing releases 'feel good' endorphins in the body.

12. Remember your "why". Why you are trying to be more positive, what your goals are, how things will be better once you meet your goals, etc.

13. Practice gratitude. When you're feeling thankful, you'll feel more positive.

14. Live in the moment. Stop worrying about yesterday or what's coming. Do what you can do today to get one step closer to reaching your goals.

15. Indulge yourself occasionally. You are working hard to be a more positive person. You deserve a small reward.

16. Carry a funny photo with you. Save a funny video on your phone to give you a boost when you're feeling down.

17. Look at each challenge as an opportunity to grow. Strive for excellence.

18. Relax. Sometimes you just need to step back, breathe deep and relax to get the good vibes flowing again.

19. Get physically active to release more 'feel good' endorphins.

20. Believe in yourself. The only thing keeping you from succeeding is your own negative thoughts. Stop getting in your own way.

21. Stop making excuses and laying blame. Take responsibility for your actions and make the choice to do better next time.

22. Observe your thought patterns. Are there certain times of the day when you're feeling more negative? What can you do to make those times more positive?

23. Ask yourself, does this really matter? Will it matter next week or next month? If not, let it go. This called not sweating the small stuff.

24. Practice proper posture. Standing or sitting up with the back straight, shoulders back and chin up will help the mind and body feel better.

25. Be kind to others. Compliment a stranger. Do something nice for coworker or friend. Call a family member you haven't talked to in a while.

26. Read something inspiring every day. Follow those who inspire you most and see what they do each day to make like the best it can be. Follow their lead.

27. Dance and sing. It doesn't matter if you have two left feet or can't carry a tune. Crank up the music and give it all you've got.

28. Look for the positive. Even in the worst of situations, there's always something positive if you just look for it.

29. Have a personal mantra. No matter what it is, these will be the words you live by each day that reminds you to be positive.

30. Meditate, do yoga, concentrate on your breathing and relaxing your mind.

Day, Date, Year

Thought Focus For Today *(Affirmation and/or Quote)*

DAILY TASKS (in order of priority)	

CONTACT TODAY

	PERSON	CONTACT INFO	REASON

CONVERSATION NOTES

Today's Success Mindset Goal Notes:

_____

_____

_____

Today's Obstacles: I dealt with these by...

_____

_____

_____

Today's Progress: I'm proud of...

_____

_____

_____

Goal Met Today! Celebration Time!

_____

_____

_____

My advice to others...

_____

_____

_____

Quote Me:
"
_____
                                        "

My Next Step is...

_____

_____

Notes & Resources

_____

_____

_____

Challenges I Will Overcome

Life is full of challenges. This worksheet is designed to help you work through how you'll overcome the challenges you face.

The Challenge I'm Currently Facing

_____

_____

_____

_____

_____

The Obstacle(s) Standing in My Way

Obstacle #1:

_____

_____

How I Will Overcome It

_____

_____

_____

_____

People & Tools I'll Need to Help Me with This

_____

_____

_____

_____

Obstacle #2:

_____

How I Will Overcome It

_____

_____

_____

_____

People & Tools I'll Need to Help Me with This

_____

_____

_____

_____

Obstacle #3:

_____

_____

How I Will Overcome It

_____

_____

_____

_____

People & Tools I'll Need to Help Me with This

_____

_____

_____

_____

Previous Challenges That May Resurface & How I Will Handle Them

_____

_____

_____

_____

_____

Previous Challenges That May Resurface & How I Will Handle Them

_____

_____

_____

_____

_____

_____

_____

More Thoughts on This Challenge:

_____

_____

_____

_____

_____

_____

_____

_____

_____

_____

_____

_____

Top Characteristics of Happy People

Ever wonder why some people always seem happy when others do not? It's all about how you view things. Below are the top characteristics of happy people.

Happy people:

- Practice gratitude and show their appreciation.
- Are genuinely nice to others
- Are open and honest
- Are cooperative
- Smile when they mean it
- Are well-adjusted and appreciate simple pleasures
- Surround themselves with other happy people
- Are spontaneous and adventurous
- Are good listeners
- Have fewer expectations, and fewer disappointments
- Don't judge others and don't let judgmental people affect them.
- Actively try to be happy each day
- Are resilient. They bounce back from obstacles and failures.
- Help others when they can
- Spend time doing nothing
- Choose meaningful conversations over small talk
- Stay connected with those they love
- Look for the positive in everything
- Regularly unplug from technology, if only for a few hours a week.
- Try to maintain a healthy mind and body through proper eating, exercise, and rest.

- Laugh loud and laugh often, fully enjoying the moment
- Like themselves
- Have self-control
- Are optimistic
- Are spiritual
- Lead a balanced life
- Embrace their creativity

S.M.A.R.T. Goals Worksheet

Goals give us something to visualize, to work towards. They keep us from becoming stagnant in life. This worksheet is designed to help you set smart goals.

Today's Date: _____   Date to Achieve Goal By: _____

Date Goal Achieved: _____

Specific: What exactly do you want to accomplish? What is the desired result. Why do you want to achieve it? How do you plan to achieve it? Be specific.

_____
_____
_____
_____
_____
_____
_____
_____
_____
_____
_____
_____
_____
_____
_____
_____
_____
_____

Measurable: How will you know when you've accomplished this goal? How are you going to measure your progress? How often are you going to measure and document your progress?

_____

_____

_____

_____

_____

_____

_____

_____

_____

_____

Achievable: Is this goal achievable? What skills, tools, and resources do you need to make it happen? Do you have these? If not, how will you get them?

_____

_____

_____

_____

_____

_____

_____

_____

_____

_____

Relevant: Is this goal relevant to your life? Will it help you reach your life goals quicker? Will it benefit your life in some way? How is it relevant? Be specific.

_____
_____
_____
_____
_____
_____
_____
_____
_____

Timely: When do you want to achieve this goal? Is this target date reasonable?

_____
_____
_____

Progress / Notes

Month 1	Month 2	Month 3	Month 4	Month 5	Month 6

Every step that I take to move forward allows me to grow stronger by the day.

10 Things I Love About Myself & Why

You have a vast amount of qualities, characteristics, talents, skills, virtues, etc., which others wish they had. Loving and appreciating your own uniqueness isn't always easy to do. When you love something about yourself, you need to know why so you can remind yourself, if needed, and continue to build your confidence.

1. I love

   because

2. I love

   because

3. I love

   because

4. I love

    because

5. I love

    because

6. I love

    because

7. I love

    because

8. I love _____

   because _____

   _____

   _____

9. I love _____

   because _____

   _____

   _____

10. I love _____

   because _____

   _____

Change Your Thinking

The goal for this worksheet is to help you open your eyes to how you really feel and to give you a starting point for where you can improve your thought process and confidence. No one else has to see this, so be honest when completing each sentence. As you progress with building your confidence, using a fresh copy of this worksheet, complete it again. Do this several times over the course of a month or two to see how you are improving.

My best friend is…

I am avoiding…

I am proud of these choices I have made…

I am willing to struggle for…

Today is going to be…

I believe that…

I connect most with….

I don't like to admit…

I feel my future is…

One small thing I wish I could change is….

One big thing I wish I could change is…

I gain strength from…

I get angry when…

One small thing I can change right now is…

One big thing I can change right now is…

I am ashamed of…

I go to work every day because…

The most important thing(s) in my life is…

I hope that…

Today I would like to…

I love when…

I make a difference in this world by…

I make excuses because…

I secretly enjoy…

I struggle when…

I thrive when…

I was really happy when…

I would never…

Today I fear that…

I'd really enjoy…

Sometimes I wish I could…

The thing I fear most is…

To make me feel fulfilled I need…

Today I believed that…

Fear has a habit of rising to the top at the most inconvenient times. Oftentimes the fear irrational and can be overcome with forethought and practice. Use this worksheet to help you work through your fears.

One thing that makes me feel nervous or scared:

When this fear is triggered, what thoughts go through your mind?

In what areas of the body do you feel the fear? How does your body react (forehead sweat, sticky palms, etc.)?

How do you respond to this fear (fight / flight / avoidance / feel depressed / etc.)?

What exactly is it that makes you fearful? Dig deep to the source and be specific.

Realistically, what are the chances of this happening?

What can you do to lessen the likelihood of it happening?

What's the worst that could happen if your fear comes to fruition?

What is the long-term cost (emotional, physical, financial, etc.) of not overcoming this fear?

If the worst-case scenario happened, how would you consciously work through it? What steps would you take?

What benefits will you receive if you work through this fear?

I can change my fixed mindsets into growth mindsets for more success.

Fixed Mindset	Growth Mindset
I am a terrible parent.	I made mistakes as a parent, **but** I tried my best.
My mistake ruined everything.	My mistake cost me some time, **but** I can learn from it.
I am a complete mess.	I do some things well and I need to improve on others.
Why even try?	I know if I try hard I will succeed at some things, **but** not everything.
Things never go my way.	Right now, things aren't going my way, **but** at other times they have
If he leaves me, I'll die.	I would like to keep my marriage, **but** many people have a happy life after a divorce and I can too.
My kid is a terrible mess.	My kid is having some problems right now, **but** I know he will learn from his mistakes.
Life is too hard.	Sometimes I don't have the energy to keep trying, **but** I take one step at a time.
I just can't do anything right.	I have trouble with some things, **but** I am good at others; for example, I am good at being a friend.
My daughter is absolutely horrible.	I don't like my daughter's behavior right now, **but** I am proud that she is so bright.
My life is a disaster.	I have had many losses, **but** many things in my life are good, including my friends and my health.
I'm *lucky* I lived.	I lived because I worked hard with my doctors and did everything they said before the surgery.
I don't deserve my job.	I have made mistakes in my job, **but** I have also made valuable contributions.
My husband/wife/partner does everything for our family.	I contribute to our family in different ways from my husband/wife.
I should support my family better.	I have supported my family for years and I can still support them, in many ways.

Notes: _____

Fixed Mindset	Growth Mindset
My divorce is entirely my fault.	I made mistakes in my marriage, but not all of the problems were my fault.
I failed at my job.	I was fired from this job, **but** I did the best I could at the time.
When I had that drink, I ruined my sobriety.	I had a lapse, **but** that doesn't mean that I'll have a full- blown relapse.
You can't trust anyone.	You can trust some people and others you cannot trust.
I should have known better than to trust him.	I am learning that I need to move slowly when learning to trust others and wait to make sure they are trustworthy.
He should be nicer to me.	I would like it if he wasn't so rude, **but** he is who he is.
I know John is mad at me because he didn't even speak.	John may be having his own problems.
My boss frowned at me; I'm going to get fired.	I don't really know why my boss frowned at me. Maybe he is having a bad day.
I just know something terrible is about to happen.	I'm worried right now, **but** that doesn't mean something bad is bound to happen.
This will never work.	This may work or not, **but** it is worth trying.
Everything will turn out bad.	Some things won't turn out the way I want, **but** others will.

Notes: _____

These mindsets and changes have special, personal meaning for me.

Mistakes are positive when I learn what to rule out he next time. I've learned a lot.

My initial thought/idea: _____

_____

My miscalculation: _____

_____

Lessons learned: _____

_____

_____

_____

_____

How my mistake helped me in the long run: _____

_____

_____

My initial thought/idea: _____

_____

My miscalculation: _____

_____

Lessons learned: _____

_____

_____

_____

_____

How my mistake helped me in the long run: _____

_____

Making the Most of a Difficult Situation

Life is full of difficult situations. How we react to them is the key to getting through most. This checklist is designed to help you work through the difficult situations you face.

1. **Assess the situation.** What created the problem. What solutions can you think of?

2. **Talk to someone** about the situation; a mentor, friend or loved one. Oftentimes having an outsider's perspective and feedback and help you develop a long-term solution.

3. **Understand that change in inevitable.** Find the courage and strength to accept it. Don't let your emotions get the best of you.

4. **Find the positive.** Look for the positive in difficult situations. Rarely is it all bad.

5. **Let go of toxic friends** and welcome new, positive ones into your life. They may have some really good ideas to help you through future difficult times. Even if they don't, you've at least let go of those who added to the negative pressure.

6. **Learn from it.** Learn from every situation. Mistakes are just stepping stones in which we learn. Every situation has something you can take from it.

7. **Keep trying.** Don't let this setback stop you from trying again in the future. You only fail once you stop trying.

8. **It's for the best.** Know that some things are for the best. It may be difficult. It may seem impossible. But focus on how things will soon be better.

9. **Communicate.** When dealing with others during tough situations, keep the lines of communication open and positive. Talk with the person. Listen to their side of things. Work together and compromise if necessary to find a solution that works for everyone.

10. **Accept the challenge.** Think of tough situations as a challenge. Be strong, keep calm and meet it head on. Find the opportunity. What can you do to make it better? What can you do to keep it from happening again?

11. **Don't dwell on it.** Most situations do not have a quick fix. While working towards the solution, don't dwell on the issue. Instead, focus on making steps towards the solution while enjoying life to its fullest.

12. **Let it go.** When it's impossible to avoid a tough situation and the solution is out of your control. Let it go. If it's a boss or job creating the problem, find a new job. Nothing is worth dealing with toxicity daily.

13. **Reflect and revisit.** Once the situation is over and you've had some time to move on from it. Revisit it. Reflect on how you reacted, what you could have done differently or better. Try to find how the issue came about, were there warning signs, did you miss something?

14. **Stay confident.** During tough times, it's easy to let our minds turn to negative thinking. Don't let this happen. Nix the self-criticism and remember this too shall pass. You are more than capable of dealing with this and coming out ahead.

15. **Stay busy.** A busy mind has less time to dwell on the negatives. Actively work every day to reach your goal. The more active you are, the quicker the solution will come.

Coping with Your Triggers

Everyone has emotional triggers that negatively affect how we react in certain situations. The trigger could be a person, situation, location, or activity. It might be a sound, smell, sight, thought or the feel of something. This worksheet is designed to help you find ways to cope with your triggers.

The trigger that sets you off:

_____

_____

_____

What emotional response does this trigger set off (feeling of shame, rage, etc.)?

_____

_____

_____

_____

_____

_____

What physical symptoms do you experience when triggered (racing heart, shaking, etc.)?

_____

_____

_____

_____

_____

_____

What negative thoughts do you have when you experience this trigger (feeling of being a failure, of hurting someone, etc.)?

_____

_____

_____

_____

_____

_____

How does your response affect others? (Do you get grumpy with family, irritated with your pets? Do you fail to finish your work, putting your team behind schedule?)

_____

_____

_____

_____

_____

_____

_____

_____

_____

_____

How can you avoid or reduce exposure to this trigger?

_____

_____

_____

_____

_____

_____

When it cannot be avoided, how do you want to deal with the situation? You can choose how you feel and react to it. (deep breath, relax, center yourself, etc.)

_____

_____

_____

_____

_____

_____

Phrases you can use to get you through the trigger without reacting. (stay calm, relax, I'm okay, I can do this, etc.) Practice these with others and by yourself so it is second nature when the trigger happens!

_____

_____

_____

_____

_____

_____

People who can help you work through the situation & help you practice.

_____

_____

_____

_____

Other Items I May Need to Help Me with This

_____

_____

_____

_____

Practicing Mindfulness

Practicing mindfulness is something that can be integrated into your life so it becomes natural. Here are some ways to get started.

- ☐ Be aware of the moment. As you wake up in the morning, during your lunch break, as you go to bed at night, any time you have a moment. What are you seeing, smelling, physically feeling, hearing? What emotions are being evoked?

- ☐ Hydrate your body mindfully. As you drink water, notice the taste, temperature and how it feels in your body.

- ☐ Watch the sun rise or set. Notice the patterns, the colors, the wind, or lack of, the way it feels on your body.

- ☐ Walk barefoot. Feel the soil between your toes, the texture of the grass, the connection you have to mother earth.

- ☐ Slow down and enjoy life. It's often the small things that make the biggest difference. Don't ignore them because you're rushing through your life.

- ☐ When eating, be aware of the scents, flavors, and textures of the foods. Pay attention to how it makes your body feel.

- ☐ When cooking, observe the processes you go through, slicing, stirring, and pouring.

- ☐ Let your mind wander while you relax and breathe deep. Using all your senses take in the things around you.

- [ ] Observe your moods. How does your body feel when you are confused, happy, sad?

- [ ] Pay attention to your actions and reactions. How do you act or react in different situations? How does that affect the rest of your day or week?

- [ ] Connect with nature. Take a walk in a park, hike a trail, visit a beach. Notice the movement of the trees and flow of water.

- [ ] At the end of each day, list 2-3 things you are grateful for.

- [ ] Start each day with intention. Set goals for each day and strive to meet them.

- [ ] Reduce life clutter and distractions. This includes negative people who hinder your happiness.

- [ ] Observe your body language. How are you projecting yourself? If you could not speak, what would your body be saying?

- [ ] Write in a journal each day. Reflect on the day. Make note of things that happened, what you thought and how you felt in the moment.

- [ ] Practice meditation daily. Add soft music or scented candles if it helps.

- [ ] Plan for tomorrow so you face it head-on with few interruptions.

- [ ] Renew or create relationships with positive people.

- [ ] Exercise. Make note of how your body felt before, during and after.

- [ ] Notice the difference in your body and mind when you wake a few minutes early or get a full nights rest.

Thinking Styles to Avoid

The way we think has a direct impact on our emotions and behaviors. While there are many styles of thinking, there are 10 thought patterns said to be more than a little problematic.

Thought Pattern		Details
Polarized Thinking (Black & White)	→	Seeing things as only having two extreme sides; black or white, good or bad, right or wrong. You leave no room for a gray area or middle ground.
Overgeneralization	→	Thinking things like "I'll *never* get this" or "this *always* happens to me". You believe the outcome of one incident will be the same outcome for all future situations. You tend to shy away from future actions based on the results of that single event.
Making Assumptions	→	You jump to conclusions, or make assumptions, without having all (or any of) the facts. You might assume you know how someone is feeling or what they're thinking.
Personalizing	→	You relate everything to you; comparing yourself to others, thinking people are reacting to you. This also encompasses blaming yourself even when something is not your fault.
Filtering	→	The opposite of seeing everything through rose-colored glasses. This is seeing only the negative part of a situation. You pick out one or two negatives and filter everything else out. You fail to recognize the positive parts of it. You only see what you want to see.
Catastrophizing	→	Blowing things out of proportion. Making them out to be much worse than they should be. You've probably heard the phrase making a mountain out of a mole hill. "We're not going!", because you're running a little behind schedule.

Unreasonable Expectations	→	Unreasonable thinking that usually involves phrases like "*I should*" or "*You must*". Thoughts that put too much pressure (or unrealistic expectations) on you or others. You expect others to change for you.
Global Labeling	→	Labeling others or yourself based on behavior displayed in an isolated or specific situation despite evidence to the contrary. Stereotyping. You might think "I'm stupid" even though you are not.
Magnifying/Minimizing	→	Devaluing yourself while raising the value of someone else. You magnify good things about others while not recognizing your own good qualities. This is more than just being humble. It's not recognizing or accepting that you have good qualities.
Emotional Reasoning	→	You let your feelings determine how you view a situation, despite evidence to the contrary. If you're feeling anxious when you get the news of an upcoming event, you might feel fear of what is going to happen. If you're feeing miserable when you hear your niece is getting married, you view it with pessimism.
Distorted Sense of Power - The Victim	→	You view and/or portray yourself as the victim, like you have no control of things happening in your life. You blame others for how you feel, problems you face, things that happen to you. You feel stuck and fail to recognize that you have control if you will just take it.
Distorted Sense of Power - The Responsible One	→	You feel you are responsible for other people's emotions. You strive to make everyone happy, to 'fix' their sadness. You spend so much time and effort trying to help others that it costs you your own happiness.
Always Being Right	→	You feel the need to prove yourself. To prove that your opinions, beliefs, or actions are right. You are uninterested in hearing a difference of opinion.

Positive Thinking To Help Situational Depression

Negativity is often an overwhelming element of situational depression. For millions of people with this type of depression, the key to begin breaking free is to change the situation, when possible, and/or the way the situation is viewed.

What situation is contributing to or causing my depression?

_____

_____

_____

_____

Is the situation a result of my actions or choices? Explain.

_____

_____

_____

_____

What are the positive things I've learned due the experience?

_____

_____

_____

_____

If I could do it over again, this is what I would do differently:

_____

_____

_____

Is negative self-talk making my depression worse? Give examples:

_____

_____

_____

_____

I can change the negative thoughts and self-talk into positives like these:

_____

_____

_____

_____

I can alleviate my stress and depression by focusing on the positives such as:

_____

_____

_____

_____

When situations are not a result of my actions or choices and I have limited control over things, I need to take these steps to maintain a positive mindset:

_____

_____

_____

_____

If I need additional help staying positive or fighting back the depression, I can count on and contact these friends and professionals:

_____

_____

25 Positive Thinking Affirmations

Affirmations are simple reminders to our subconscious that tells it to stay positive and focused on reaching our goals. They are meant to be used for ourselves, not for others. Affirmations can create more appreciation for the things we have and are surrounded with. They can bring more joy and happiness to our lives.

When creating your affirmations, there are a few things to keep in mind.

- Including the words "I am" in your affirmations bring power to your statement.

- Positively state what you want, not what you don't want.

- Keep your statements short and specific.

- Include words that show action or emotion

- Before stating your affirmation, take a deep breath and focus on what you're saying.

- Be grateful for what you have, the people in your life and your surroundings.

- Let go of the past. You can't change it so don't waste time thinking on it.

- Celebrate your 'wins'.

Below are 25 positive thinking affirmations to get you started.

26. I can do better, just by deciding to do so.

27. Life is what I make of it.

28. I can.

29. I am above negative thoughts and actions.

30. Happiness is a choice. I choose it.

31. Today, I let go of old habits and take up new ones.

32. I am conquering obstacles every day.

33. I am seeing a positive in every situation.

34. My thoughts are becoming more positive each day.

35. Life is getting better all the time.

36. I am turning into the person I always wanted to be.

37. Thinking positive is starting to feel more natural to me.

38. My optimism is altering my reality.

39. I am at peace with my past and looking forward to the future.

40. I no longer fear tomorrow.

41. I am blessed.

42. This too shall pass.

43. I control how I feel.

44. I am willing to do what it takes to make positive changes.

45. The future is mine, if I choose to take it.

46. I am indestructible.

47. This moment is awesome.

48. Positive thinking is part of who I am now.

49. Today is the first day of my new life.

50. Everything happens for a reason that serves me.

Every step that I take to move forward allows me to grow stronger by the day.

30 Ways to Think More Positively

After years of having a fixed, negative mindset, it's tough to change one's ways. But with practice, you can create a more positive outlook on life. Here's 30 ways to practice thinking more positively.

31. When talking, replace negative words with positive words. Instead of saying "This is too hard", say "I can do this" or "I accept this challenge".

32. When thinking, use empowering words; those that make you feel strong, happy, motivated and in control.

33. Journal your thoughts. Celebrate your successes. Document and analyze the losses. Find where you went wrong and plan to do better next time. Learn from your mistakes.

34. Counter each negative thought with multiple positive thoughts. When you catch yourself having negative thoughts, take a moment to think two or three positive thoughts.

35. Go somewhere that brings you peace and happiness. This might be a nature walk, a quiet place like a museum that is visually appealing, an area where you listen to music, a park where you can watch kids and pets play happily. As often as possible, visit this place where you feel peace and happiness.

36. Practice positive affirmations. The more you practice, the easier it will become.

37. Forgive yourself for missteps. It happens. The important this is not to dwell on them and keep moving forward.

38. Surround yourself with positive people.

39. Add inspiring visuals and colors to your home and work space.

40.   Look at things from a different point of view. When you can see both sides, you can eliminate a lot of negatively.

41. Laugh aloud and often. There's always something to laugh about. Smiling and laughing releases 'feel good' endorphins in the body.

42. Remember your "why". Why you are trying to be more positive, what your goals are, how things will be better once you meet your goals, etc.

43. Practice gratitude. When you're feeling thankful, you'll feel more positive.

44. Live in the moment. Stop worrying about yesterday or what's coming. Do what you can do today to get one step closer to reaching your goals.

45. Indulge yourself occasionally. You are working hard to be a more positive person. You deserve a small reward.

46. Carry a funny photo with you. Save a funny video on your phone to give you a boost when you're feeling down.

47. Look at each challenge as an opportunity to grow. Strive for excellence.

48. Relax. Sometimes you just need to step back, breathe deep and relax to get the good vibes flowing again.

49. Get physically active to release more 'feel good' endorphins.

50.   Believe in yourself. The only thing keeping you from succeeding is your own negative thoughts. Stop getting in your own way.

51. Stop making excuses and laying blame. Take responsibility for your actions and make the choice to do better next time.

52. Observe your thought patterns. Are there certain times of the day when you're feeling more negative? What can you do to make those times more positive?

53. Ask yourself, does this really matter? Will it matter next week or next month? If not, let it go. This called not sweating the small stuff.

54. Practice proper posture. Standing or sitting up with the back straight, shoulders back and chin up will help the mind and body feel better.

55. Be kind to others. Compliment a stranger. Do something nice for coworker or friend. Call a family member you haven't talked to in a while.

56. Read something inspiring every day. Follow those who inspire you most and see what they do each day to make like the best it can be. Follow their lead.

57. Dance and sing. It doesn't matter if you have two left feet or can't carry a tune. Crank up the music and give it all you've got.

58. Look for the positive. Even in the worst of situations, there's always something positive if you just look for it.

59. Have a personal mantra. No matter what it is, these will be the words you live by each day that reminds you to be positive.

60. Meditate, do yoga, concentrate on your breathing and relaxing your mind.

Day, Date, Year

Thought Focus For Today *(Affirmation and/or Quote)*

DAILY TASKS (in order of priority)	

CONTACT TODAY

	PERSON	CONTACT INFO	REASON

CONVERSATION NOTES

Today's Success Mindset Goal Notes:

_____
_____
_____

Today's Obstacles: I dealt with these by...

_____
_____
_____

Today's Progress: I'm proud of...

_____
_____
_____

Goal Met Today! Celebration Time!

_____
_____

My advice to others...

_____
_____
_____

Quote Me:
"_____
_____"

My Next Step is...

_____
_____

Notes & Resources

_____
_____
_____

Challenges I Will Overcome

Life is full of challenges. This worksheet is designed to help you work through how you'll overcome the challenges you face.

The Challenge I'm Currently Facing

_____

_____

_____

_____

_____

The Obstacle(s) Standing in My Way

Obstacle #1:

_____

_____

How I Will Overcome It

_____

_____

_____

_____

People & Tools I'll Need to Help Me with This

_____

_____

_____

_____

Obstacle #2:

_____

How I Will Overcome It

_____

_____

_____

_____

People & Tools I'll Need to Help Me with This

_____

_____

_____

_____

Obstacle #3:

_____

_____

How I Will Overcome It

_____

_____

_____

_____

People & Tools I'll Need to Help Me with This

_____

_____

_____

_____

Previous Challenges That May Resurface & How I Will Handle Them

_____

_____

_____

_____

_____

Previous Challenges That May Resurface & How I Will Handle Them

_____

_____

_____

_____

_____

_____

_____

_____

More Thoughts on This Challenge:

_____

_____

_____

_____

_____

_____

_____

_____

_____

_____

_____

_____

_____

Top Characteristics of Happy People

Ever wonder why some people always seem happy when others do not? It's all about how you view things. Below are the top characteristics of happy people.

Happy people:

- Practice gratitude and show their appreciation.
- Are genuinely nice to others
- Are open and honest
- Are cooperative
- Smile when they mean it
- Are well-adjusted and appreciate simple pleasures
- Surround themselves with other happy people
- Are spontaneous and adventurous
- Are good listeners
- Have fewer expectations, and fewer disappointments
- Don't judge others and don't let judgmental people affect them.
- Actively try to be happy each day
- Are resilient. They bounce back from obstacles and failures.
- Help others when they can
- Spend time doing nothing
- Choose meaningful conversations over small talk
- Stay connected with those they love
- Look for the positive in everything
- Regularly unplug from technology, if only for a few hours a week.
- Try to maintain a healthy mind and body through proper eating, exercise, and rest.

- Laugh loud and laugh often, fully enjoying the moment
- Like themselves
- Have self-control
- Are optimistic
- Are spiritual
- Lead a balanced life
- Embrace their creativity

S.M.A.R.T. Goals Worksheet

Goals give us something to visualize, to work towards. They keep us from becoming stagnant in life. This worksheet is designed to help you set smart goals.

Today's Date: _____   Date to Achieve Goal By: _____

Date Goal Achieved: _____

Specific: What exactly do you want to accomplish? What is the desired result. Why do you want to achieve it? How do you plan to achieve it? Be specific.

_____

_____

_____

_____

_____

_____

_____

_____

_____

_____

_____

_____

_____

_____

_____

_____

_____

Measurable: How will you know when you've accomplished this goal? How are you going to measure your progress? How often are you going to measure and document your progress?

_____

_____

_____

_____

_____

_____

_____

_____

_____

_____

_____

_____

Achievable: Is this goal achievable? What skills, tools, and resources do you need to make it happen? Do you have these? If not, how will you get them?

_____

_____

_____

_____

_____

_____

_____

_____

_____

_____

_____

Relevant: Is this goal relevant to your life? Will it help you reach your life goals quicker? Will it benefit your life in some way? How is it relevant? Be specific.

_____

_____

_____

_____

_____

_____

_____

_____

_____

_____

Timely: When do you want to achieve this goal? Is this target date reasonable?

_____

_____

_____

Progress / Notes

Month 1	Month 2	Month 3	Month 4	Month 5	Month 6

Every step that I take to move forward allows me to grow stronger by the day.

10 Things I Love About Myself & Why

You have a vast amount of qualities, characteristics, talents, skills, virtues, etc., which others wish they had. Loving and appreciating your own uniqueness isn't always easy to do. When you love something about yourself, you need to know why so you can remind yourself, if needed, and continue to build your confidence.

11. I love

because

12. I love

because

13. I love

because

14. I love

   because

15. I love

   because

16. I love

   because

17. I love

   because

18. I love

because

19. I love

because

20. I love

because

Change Your Thinking

The goal for this worksheet is to help you open your eyes to how you really feel and to give you a starting point for where you can improve your thought process and confidence. No one else has to see this, so be honest when completing each sentence. As you progress with building your confidence, using a fresh copy of this worksheet, complete it again. Do this several times over the course of a month or two to see how you are improving.

My best friend is…

I am avoiding…

I am proud of these choices I have made…

I am willing to struggle for…

Today is going to be…

I believe that…

I connect most with….

I don't like to admit…

I feel my future is…

One small thing I wish I could change is….

One big thing I wish I could change is…

I gain strength from…

I get angry when…

One small thing I can change right now is…

One big thing I can change right now is…

I am ashamed of…

I go to work every day because…

The most important thing(s) in my life is…

I hope that…

Today I would like to…

I love when…

I make a difference in this world by…

I make excuses because…

I secretly enjoy…

I struggle when…

I thrive when…

I was really happy when…

I would never…

Today I fear that…

I'd really enjoy…

Sometimes I wish I could…

The thing I fear most is…

To make me feel fulfilled I need…

Today I believed that…

Fear has a habit of rising to the top at the most inconvenient times. Oftentimes the fear irrational and can be overcome with forethought and practice. Use this worksheet to help you work through your fears.

One thing that makes me feel nervous or scared:

_____

_____

_____

When this fear is triggered, what thoughts go through your mind?

_____

_____

_____

_____

_____

In what areas of the body do you feel the fear? How does your body react (forehead sweat, sticky palms, etc.)?

_____

_____

_____

_____

_____

_____

How do you respond to this fear (fight / flight / avoidance / feel depressed / etc.)?

What exactly is it that makes you fearful? Dig deep to the source and be specific.

Realistically, what are the chances of this happening?

What can you do to lessen the likelihood of it happening?

What's the worst that could happen if your fear comes to fruition?

What is the long-term cost (emotional, physical, financial, etc.) of not overcoming this fear?

If the worst-case scenario happened, how would you consciously work through it? What steps would you take?

What benefits will you receive if you work through this fear?

I can change my fixed mindsets into growth mindsets for more success.

Fixed Mindset	Growth Mindset
I am a terrible parent.	I made mistakes as a parent, **but** I tried my best.
My mistake ruined everything.	My mistake cost me some time, **but** I can learn from it.
I am a complete mess.	I do some things well and I need to improve on others.
Why even try?	I know if I try hard I will succeed at some things, **but** not everything.
Things never go my way.	Right now, things aren't going my way, **but** at other times they have
If he leaves me, I'll die.	I would like to keep my marriage, **but** many people have a happy life after a divorce and I can too.
My kid is a terrible mess.	My kid is having some problems right now, **but** I know he will learn from his mistakes.
Life is too hard.	Sometimes I don't have the energy to keep trying, **but** I take one step at a time.
I just can't do anything right.	I have trouble with some things, **but** I am good at others; for example, I am good at being a friend.
My daughter is absolutely horrible.	I don't like my daughter's behavior right now, **but** I am proud that she is so bright.
My life is a disaster.	I have had many losses, **but** many things in my life are good, including my friends and my health.
I'm *lucky* I lived.	I lived because I worked hard with my doctors and did everything they said before the surgery.
I don't deserve my job.	I have made mistakes in my job, **but** I have also made valuable contributions.
My husband/wife/partner does everything for our family.	I contribute to our family in different ways from my husband/wife.
I should support my family better.	I have supported my family for years and I can still support them, in many ways.

Notes:

Fixed Mindset	Growth Mindset
My divorce is entirely my fault.	I made mistakes in my marriage, but not all of the problems were my fault.
I failed at my job.	I was fired from this job, **but** I did the best I could at the time.
When I had that drink, I ruined my sobriety.	I had a lapse, **but** that doesn't mean that I'll have a full- blown relapse.
You can't trust anyone.	You can trust some people and others you cannot trust.
I should have known better than to trust him.	I am learning that I need to move slowly when learning to trust others and wait to make sure they are trustworthy.
He should be nicer to me.	I would like it if he wasn't so rude, **but** he is who he is.
I know John is mad at me because he didn't even speak.	John may be having his own problems.
My boss frowned at me; I'm going to get fired.	I don't really know why my boss frowned at me. Maybe he is having a bad day.
I just know something terrible is about to happen.	I'm worried right now, **but** that doesn't mean something bad is bound to happen.
This will never work.	This may work or not, **but** it is worth trying.
Everything will turn out bad.	Some things won't turn out the way I want, **but** others will.

Notes: _____

These mindsets and changes have special, personal meaning for me.

Mistakes are positive when I learn what to rule out he next time. I've learned a lot.

My initial thought/idea: _____

_____

My miscalculation: _____

_____

Lessons learned: _____

_____

_____

_____

_____

How my mistake helped me in the long run: _____

_____

_____

My initial thought/idea: _____

_____

My miscalculation: _____

_____

Lessons learned: _____

_____

_____

_____

_____

How my mistake helped me in the long run: _____

Making the Most of a Difficult Situation

Life is full of difficult situations. How we react to them is the key to getting through most. This checklist is designed to help you work through the difficult situations you face.

16. **Assess the situation.** What created the problem. What solutions can you think of?

17. **Talk to someone** about the situation; a mentor, friend or loved one. Oftentimes having an outsider's perspective and feedback and help you develop a long-term solution.

18. **Understand that change in inevitable.** Find the courage and strength to accept it. Don't let your emotions get the best of you.

19. **Find the positive.** Look for the positive in difficult situations. Rarely is it all bad.

20. **Let go of toxic friends** and welcome new, positive ones into your life. They may have some really good ideas to help you through future difficult times. Even if they don't, you've at least let go of those who added to the negative pressure.

21. **Learn from it.** Learn from every situation. Mistakes are just stepping stones in which we learn. Every situation has something you can take from it.

22. **Keep trying.** Don't let this setback stop you from trying again in the future. You only fail once you stop trying.

23. **It's for the best.** Know that some things are for the best. It may be difficult. It may seem impossible. But focus on how things will soon be better.

24. **Communicate.** When dealing with others during tough situations, keep the lines of communication open and positive. Talk with the person. Listen to their side of things. Work together and compromise if necessary to find a solution that works for everyone.

25. **Accept the challenge.** Think of tough situations as a challenge. Be strong, keep calm and meet it head on. Find the opportunity. What can you do to make it better? What can you do to keep it from happening again?

26. **Don't dwell on it.** Most situations do not have a quick fix. While working towards the solution, don't dwell on the issue. Instead, focus on making steps towards the solution while enjoying life to its fullest.

27. **Let it go.** When it's impossible to avoid a tough situation and the solution is out of your control. Let it go. If it's a boss or job creating the problem, find a new job. Nothing is worth dealing with toxicity daily.

28. **Reflect and revisit.** Once the situation is over and you've had some time to move on from it. Revisit it. Reflect on how you reacted, what you could have done differently or better. Try to find how the issue came about, were there warning signs, did you miss something?

29. **Stay confident.** During tough times, it's easy to let our minds turn to negative thinking. Don't let this happen. Nix the self-criticism and remember this too shall pass. You are more than capable of dealing with this and coming out ahead.

30. **Stay busy.** A busy mind has less time to dwell on the negatives. Actively work every day to reach your goal. The more active you are, the quicker the solution will come.

Coping with Your Triggers

Everyone has emotional triggers that negatively affect how we react in certain situations. The trigger could be a person, situation, location, or activity. It might be a sound, smell, sight, thought or the feel of something. This worksheet is designed to help you find ways to cope with your triggers.

The trigger that sets you off:

_____

_____

_____

What emotional response does this trigger set off (feeling of shame, rage, etc.)?

_____

_____

_____

_____

_____

_____

What physical symptoms do you experience when triggered (racing heart, shaking, etc.)?

_____

_____

_____

_____

_____

_____

What negative thoughts do you have when you experience this trigger (feeling of being a failure, of hurting someone, etc.)?

_____

_____

_____

_____

_____

_____

How does your response affect others? (Do you get grumpy with family, irritated with your pets? Do you fail to finish your work, putting your team behind schedule?)

_____

_____

_____

_____

_____

_____

_____

_____

_____

_____

How can you avoid or reduce exposure to this trigger?

_____

_____

_____

_____

_____

_____

When it cannot be avoided, how do you want to deal with the situation? You can choose how you feel and react to it. (deep breath, relax, center yourself, etc.)

_____

_____

_____

_____

_____

_____

Phrases you can use to get you through the trigger without reacting. (stay calm, relax, I'm okay, I can do this, etc.) Practice these with others and by yourself so it is second nature when the trigger happens!

_____

_____

_____

_____

_____

_____

People who can help you work through the situation & help you practice.

_____

_____

_____

_____

_____

Other Items I May Need to Help Me with This

_____

_____

_____

_____

Practicing Mindfulness

Practicing mindfulness is something that can be integrated into your life so it becomes natural. Here are some ways to get started.

- ☐ Be aware of the moment. As you wake up in the morning, during your lunch break, as you go to bed at night, any time you have a moment. What are you seeing, smelling, physically feeling, hearing? What emotions are being evoked?

- ☐ Hydrate your body mindfully. As you drink water, notice the taste, temperature and how it feels in your body.

- ☐ Watch the sun rise or set. Notice the patterns, the colors, the wind, or lack of, the way it feels on your body.

- ☐ Walk barefoot. Feel the soil between your toes, the texture of the grass, the connection you have to mother earth.

- ☐ Slow down and enjoy life. It's often the small things that make the biggest difference. Don't ignore them because you're rushing through your life.

- ☐ When eating, be aware of the scents, flavors, and textures of the foods. Pay attention to how it makes your body feel.

- ☐ When cooking, observe the processes you go through, slicing, stirring, and pouring.

- ☐ Let your mind wander while you relax and breathe deep. Using all your senses take in the things around you.

- [ ] Observe your moods. How does your body feel when you are confused, happy, sad?

- [ ] Pay attention to your actions and reactions. How do you act or react in different situations? How does that affect the rest of your day or week?

- [ ] Connect with nature. Take a walk in a park, hike a trail, visit a beach. Notice the movement of the trees and flow of water.

- [ ] At the end of each day, list 2-3 things you are grateful for.

- [ ] Start each day with intention. Set goals for each day and strive to meet them.

- [ ] Reduce life clutter and distractions. This includes negative people who hinder your happiness.

- [ ] Observe your body language. How are you projecting yourself? If you could not speak, what would your body be saying?

- [ ] Write in a journal each day. Reflect on the day. Make note of things that happened, what you thought and how you felt in the moment.

- [ ] Practice meditation daily. Add soft music or scented candles if it helps.

- [ ] Plan for tomorrow so you face it head-on with few interruptions.

- [ ] Renew or create relationships with positive people.

- [ ] Exercise. Make note of how your body felt before, during and after.

- [ ] Notice the difference in your body and mind when you wake a few minutes early or get a full nights rest.

Thinking Styles to Avoid

The way we think has a direct impact on our emotions and behaviors. While there are many styles of thinking, there are 10 thought patterns said to be more than a little problematic.

Thought Pattern		Details
Polarized Thinking (Black & White)	→	Seeing things as only having two extreme sides; black or white, good or bad, right or wrong. You leave no room for a gray area or middle ground.
Overgeneralization	→	Thinking things like "I'll **never** get this" or "this **always** happens to me". You believe the outcome of one incident will be the same outcome for all future situations. You tend to shy away from future actions based on the results of that single event.
Making Assumptions	→	You jump to conclusions, or make assumptions, without having all (or any of) the facts. You might assume you know how someone is feeling or what they're thinking.
Personalizing	→	You relate everything to you; comparing yourself to others, thinking people are reacting to you. This also encompasses blaming yourself even when something is not your fault.
Filtering	→	The opposite of seeing everything through rose-colored glasses. This is seeing only the negative part of a situation. You pick out one or two negatives and filter everything else out. You fail to recognize the positive parts of it. You only see what you want to see.
Catastrophizing	→	Blowing things out of proportion. Making them out to be much worse than they should be. You've probably heard the phrase making a mountain out of a mole hill. "We're not going!", because you're running a little behind schedule.

Unreasonable Expectations	→	Unreasonable thinking that usually involves phrases like "*I should*" or "*You must*". Thoughts that put too much pressure (or unrealistic expectations) on you or others. You expect others to change for you.
Global Labeling	→	Labeling others or yourself based on behavior displayed in an isolated or specific situation despite evidence to the contrary. Stereotyping. You might think "I'm stupid" even though you are not.
Magnifying/Minimizing	→	Devaluing yourself while raising the value of someone else. You magnify good things about others while not recognizing your own good qualities. This is more than just being humble. It's not recognizing or accepting that you have good qualities.
Emotional Reasoning	→	You let your feelings determine how you view a situation, despite evidence to the contrary. If you're feeling anxious when you get the news of an upcoming event, you might feel fear of what is going to happen. If you're feeing miserable when you hear your niece is getting married, you view it with pessimism.
Distorted Sense of Power - The Victim	→	You view and/or portray yourself as the victim, like you have no control of things happening in your life. You blame others for how you feel, problems you face, things that happen to you. You feel stuck and fail to recognize that you have control if you will just take it.
Distorted Sense of Power - The Responsible One	→	You feel you are responsible for other people's emotions. You strive to make everyone happy, to 'fix' their sadness. You spend so much time and effort trying to help others that it costs you your own happiness.
Always Being Right	→	You feel the need to prove yourself. To prove that your opinions, beliefs, or actions are right. You are uninterested in hearing a difference of opinion.

Positive Thinking To Help Situational Depression

Negativity is often an overwhelming element of situational depression. For millions of people with this type of depression, the key to begin breaking free is to change the situation, when possible, and/or the way the situation is viewed.

What situation is contributing to or causing my depression?

_____
_____
_____
_____

Is the situation a result of my actions or choices? Explain.

_____
_____
_____
_____

What are the positive things I've learned due the experience?

_____
_____
_____
_____

If I could do it over again, this is what I would do differently:

_____
_____

_____

Is negative self-talk making my depression worse? Give examples:

_____

_____

_____

_____

I can change the negative thoughts and self-talk into positives like these:

_____

_____

_____

_____

I can alleviate my stress and depression by focusing on the positives such as:

_____

_____

_____

_____

When situations are not a result of my actions or choices and I have limited control over things, I need to take these steps to maintain a positive mindset:

_____

_____

_____

_____

If I need additional help staying positive or fighting back the depression, I can count on and contact these friends and professionals:

_____

_____

25 Positive Thinking Affirmations

Affirmations are simple reminders to our subconscious that tells it to stay positive and focused on reaching our goals. They are meant to be used for ourselves, not for others. Affirmations can create more appreciation for the things we have and are surrounded with. They can bring more joy and happiness to our lives.

When creating your affirmations, there are a few things to keep in mind.

- Including the words "I am" in your affirmations bring power to your statement.

- Positively state what you want, not what you don't want.

- Keep your statements short and specific.

- Include words that show action or emotion

- Before stating your affirmation, take a deep breath and focus on what you're saying.

- Be grateful for what you have, the people in your life and your surroundings.

- Let go of the past. You can't change it so don't waste time thinking on it.

- Celebrate your 'wins'.

Below are 25 positive thinking affirmations to get you started.

51. I can do better, just by deciding to do so.

52. Life is what I make of it.

53. I can.

54. I am above negative thoughts and actions.

55. Happiness is a choice. I choose it.

56. Today, I let go of old habits and take up new ones.

57. I am conquering obstacles every day.

58. I am seeing a positive in every situation.

59. My thoughts are becoming more positive each day.

60. Life is getting better all the time.

61. I am turning into the person I always wanted to be.

62. Thinking positive is starting to feel more natural to me.

63. My optimism is altering my reality.

64. I am at peace with my past and looking forward to the future.

65. I no longer fear tomorrow.

66. I am blessed.

67. This too shall pass.

68. I control how I feel.

69. I am willing to do what it takes to make positive changes.

70. The future is mine, if I choose to take it.

71. I am indestructible.

72. This moment is awesome.

73. Positive thinking is part of who I am now.

74. Today is the first day of my new life.

75. Everything happens for a reason that serves me.

Every step that I take to move forward allows me to grow stronger by the day.

30 Ways to Think More Positively

After years of having a fixed, negative mindset, it's tough to change one's ways. But with practice, you can create a more positive outlook on life. Here's 30 ways to practice thinking more positively.

61. When talking, replace negative words with positive words. Instead of saying "This is too hard", say "I can do this" or "I accept this challenge".

62. When thinking, use empowering words; those that make you feel strong, happy, motivated and in control.

63. Journal your thoughts. Celebrate your successes. Document and analyze the losses. Find where you went wrong and plan to do better next time. Learn from your mistakes.

64. Counter each negative thought with multiple positive thoughts. When you catch yourself having negative thoughts, take a moment to think two or three positive thoughts.

65. Go somewhere that brings you peace and happiness. This might be a nature walk, a quiet place like a museum that is visually appealing, an area where you listen to music, a park where you can watch kids and pets play happily. As often as possible, visit this place where you feel peace and happiness.

66. Practice positive affirmations. The more you practice, the easier it will become.

67. Forgive yourself for missteps. It happens. The important this is not to dwell on them and keep moving forward.

68. Surround yourself with positive people.

69. Add inspiring visuals and colors to your home and work space.

70. Look at things from a different point of view. When you can see both sides, you can eliminate a lot of negatively.

71. Laugh aloud and often. There's always something to laugh about. Smiling and laughing releases 'feel good' endorphins in the body.

72. Remember your "why". Why you are trying to be more positive, what your goals are, how things will be better once you meet your goals, etc.

73. Practice gratitude. When you're feeling thankful, you'll feel more positive.

74. Live in the moment. Stop worrying about yesterday or what's coming. Do what you can do today to get one step closer to reaching your goals.

75. Indulge yourself occasionally. You are working hard to be a more positive person. You deserve a small reward.

76. Carry a funny photo with you. Save a funny video on your phone to give you a boost when you're feeling down.

77. Look at each challenge as an opportunity to grow. Strive for excellence.

78. Relax. Sometimes you just need to step back, breathe deep and relax to get the good vibes flowing again.

79. Get physically active to release more 'feel good' endorphins.

80. Believe in yourself. The only thing keeping you from succeeding is your own negative thoughts. Stop getting in your own way.

81. Stop making excuses and laying blame. Take responsibility for your actions and make the choice to do better next time.

82. Observe your thought patterns. Are there certain times of the day when you're feeling more negative? What can you do to make those times more positive?

83. Ask yourself, does this really matter? Will it matter next week or next month? If not, let it go. This called not sweating the small stuff.

84. Practice proper posture. Standing or sitting up with the back straight, shoulders back and chin up will help the mind and body feel better.

85. Be kind to others. Compliment a stranger. Do something nice for coworker or friend. Call a family member you haven't talked to in a while.

86. Read something inspiring every day. Follow those who inspire you most and see what they do each day to make like the best it can be. Follow their lead.

87. Dance and sing. It doesn't matter if you have two left feet or can't carry a tune. Crank up the music and give it all you've got.

88. Look for the positive. Even in the worst of situations, there's always something positive if you just look for it.

89. Have a personal mantra. No matter what it is, these will be the words you live by each day that reminds you to be positive.

90. Meditate, do yoga, concentrate on your breathing and relaxing your mind.

Day, Date, Year

Thought Focus For Today (Affirmation and/or Quote)

_____

_____

_____

DAILY TASKS (in order of priority)	

CONTACT TODAY

	PERSON	CONTACT INFO	REASON

CONVERSATION NOTES

_____

_____

_____

Today's Success Mindset Goal Notes:

_____

_____

Today's Obstacles: I dealt with these by…

_____

_____

Today's Progress: I'm proud of…

_____

_____

Goal Met Today! Celebration Time!

_____

_____

My advice to others…

_____

_____

Quote Me:
"
_____
                              "

My Next Step is…

_____

_____

Notes & Resources

_____

_____

_____

Challenges I Will Overcome

Life is full of challenges. This worksheet is designed to help you work through how you'll overcome the challenges you face.

The Challenge I'm Currently Facing

_____

_____

_____

_____

_____

The Obstacle(s) Standing in My Way

Obstacle #1:

_____

_____

How I Will Overcome It

_____

_____

_____

_____

People & Tools I'll Need to Help Me with This

_____

_____

_____

_____

Obstacle #2:

_____

How I Will Overcome It

_____

_____

_____

_____

People & Tools I'll Need to Help Me with This

_____

_____

_____

_____

Obstacle #3:

_____

_____

How I Will Overcome It

_____

_____

_____

_____

People & Tools I'll Need to Help Me with This

_____

_____

_____

_____

Previous Challenges That May Resurface & How I Will Handle Them

_____

_____

_____

_____

_____

Previous Challenges That May Resurface & How I Will Handle Them

_____

_____

_____

_____

_____

_____

_____

More Thoughts on This Challenge:

_____

_____

_____

_____

_____

_____

_____

_____

_____

_____

_____

_____

_____

Top Characteristics of Happy People

Ever wonder why some people always seem happy when others do not? It's all about how you view things. Below are the top characteristics of happy people.

Happy people:

- Practice gratitude and show their appreciation.
- Are genuinely nice to others
- Are open and honest
- Are cooperative
- Smile when they mean it
- Are well-adjusted and appreciate simple pleasures
- Surround themselves with other happy people
- Are spontaneous and adventurous
- Are good listeners
- Have fewer expectations, and fewer disappointments
- Don't judge others and don't let judgmental people affect them.
- Actively try to be happy each day
- Are resilient. They bounce back from obstacles and failures.
- Help others when they can
- Spend time doing nothing
- Choose meaningful conversations over small talk
- Stay connected with those they love
- Look for the positive in everything
- Regularly unplug from technology, if only for a few hours a week.
- Try to maintain a healthy mind and body through proper eating, exercise, and rest.

- Laugh loud and laugh often, fully enjoying the moment
- Like themselves
- Have self-control
- Are optimistic
- Are spiritual
- Lead a balanced life
- Embrace their creativity

S.M.A.R.T. Goals Worksheet

Goals give us something to visualize, to work towards. They keep us from becoming stagnant in life. This worksheet is designed to help you set smart goals.

Today's Date: _____   Date to Achieve Goal By: _____

Date Goal Achieved: _____

Specific: What exactly do you want to accomplish? What is the desired result. Why do you want to achieve it? How do you plan to achieve it? Be specific.

_____

_____

_____

_____

_____

_____

_____

_____

_____

_____

_____

_____

_____

_____

_____

_____

_____

Measurable: How will you know when you've accomplished this goal? How are you going to measure your progress? How often are you going to measure and document your progress?

_____

_____

_____

_____

_____

_____

_____

_____

_____

_____

_____

Achievable: Is this goal achievable? What skills, tools, and resources do you need to make it happen? Do you have these? If not, how will you get them?

_____

_____

_____

_____

_____

_____

_____

_____

_____

_____

_____

Relevant: Is this goal relevant to your life? Will it help you reach your life goals quicker? Will it benefit your life in some way? How is it relevant? Be specific.

_____

_____

_____

_____

_____

_____

_____

_____

_____

Timely: When do you want to achieve this goal? Is this target date reasonable?

_____

_____

_____

Progress / Notes

Month 1	Month 2	Month 3	Month 4	Month 5	Month 6

Every step that I take to move forward allows me to grow stronger by the day.

10 Things I Love About Myself & Why

ᒋᒉᒋᒉᒋᒉᒋᒉᒋᒉᒋᒉᒋᒉᒋᒉᒋᒉ

You have a vast amount of qualities, characteristics, talents, skills, virtues, etc., which others wish they had. Loving and appreciating your own uniqueness isn't always easy to do. When you love something about yourself, you need to know why so you can remind yourself, if needed, and continue to build your confidence.

21. I love

    because

22. I love

    because

23. I love

    because

24. I love

  because

25. I love

  because

26. I love

  because

27. I love

  because

28. I love

because

29. I love

because

30. I love

because

Change Your Thinking

The goal for this worksheet is to help you open your eyes to how you really feel and to give you a starting point for where you can improve your thought process and confidence. No one else has to see this, so be honest when completing each sentence. As you progress with building your confidence, using a fresh copy of this worksheet, complete it again. Do this several times over the course of a month or two to see how you are improving.

My best friend is…

I am avoiding…

I am proud of these choices I have made…

I am willing to struggle for…

Today is going to be…

I believe that…

I connect most with….

I don't like to admit…

I feel my future is…

One small thing I wish I could change is….

One big thing I wish I could change is…

I gain strength from…

I get angry when…

One small thing I can change right now is…

Made in the USA
Las Vegas, NV
22 September 2024

95634248R00070